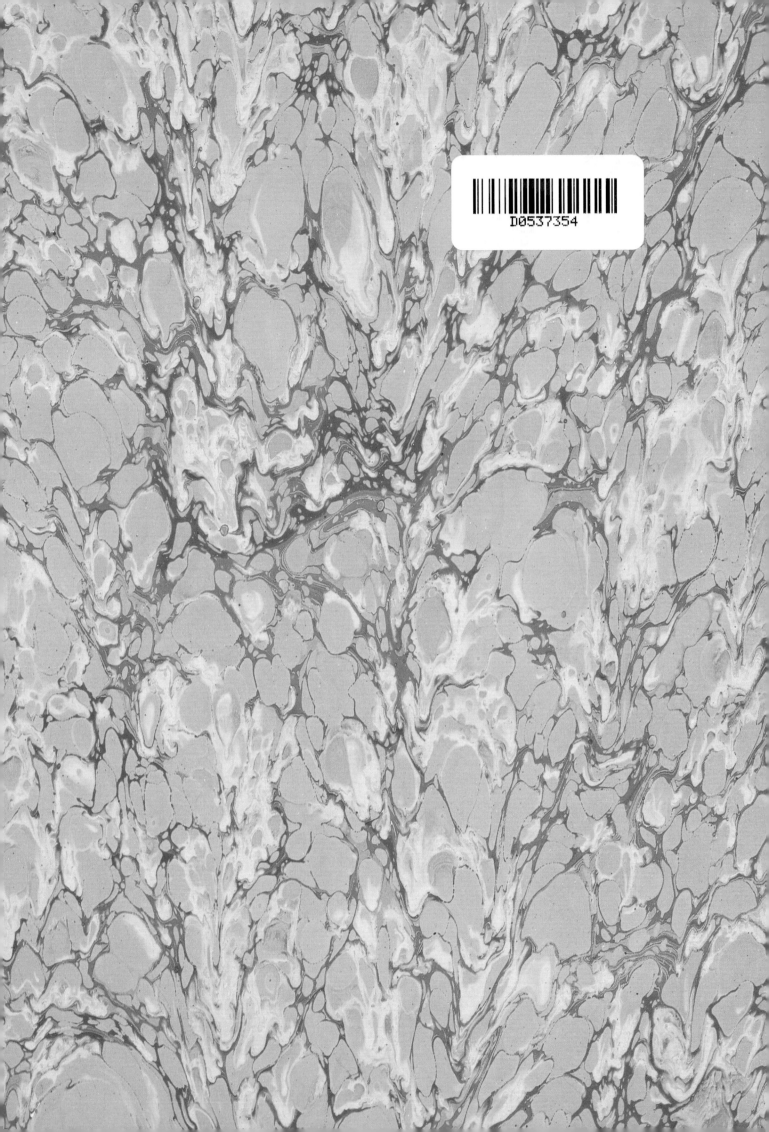

THE ISLE OF MULL

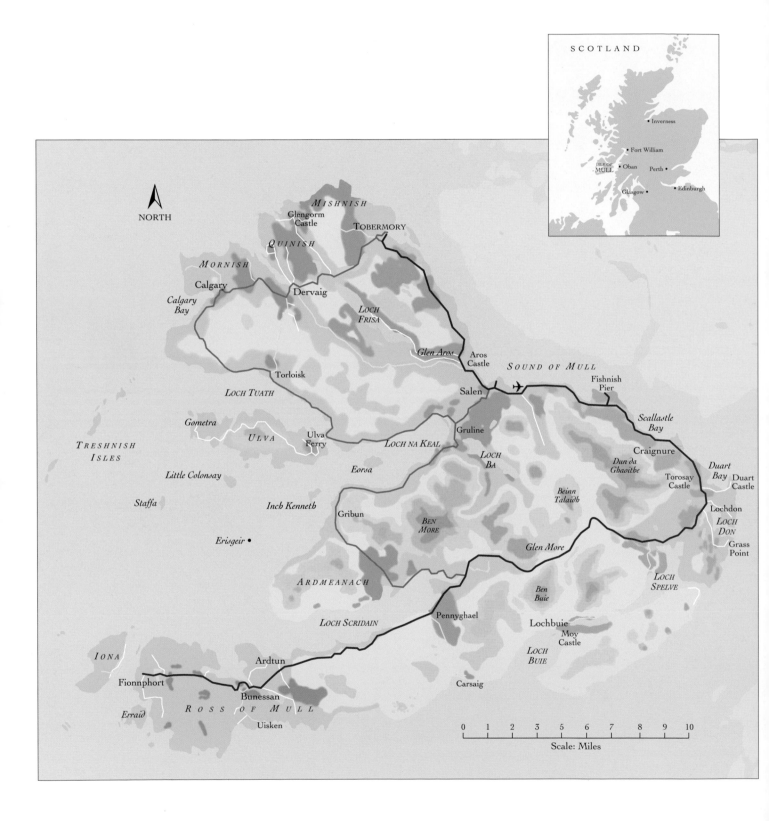

SCOTLAND

- Inverness
- Fort William
- Oban
- Perth
- ISLE OF MULL
- Glasgow
- Edinburgh

NORTH

MISHNISH

Glengorm Castle

TOBERMORY

QUINISH

MORNISH

Calgary

Dervaig

Calgary Bay

LOCH FRISA

Glen Aros

Aros Castle

SOUND OF MULL

Salen

Fishnish Pier

Torloisk

Scallastle Bay

LOCH TUATH

Gruline

Gometra

Ulva Ferry

LOCH NA KEAL

ULVA

Craignure

LOCH BA

Dun da Ghaoithe

Duart Bay

Eorsa

TRESHNISH ISLES

Little Colonsay

Torosay Castle

Duart Castle

Lochdon

Inch Kenneth

Gribun

Beinn Talaidh

LOCH DON

Staffa

Erisgeir •

BEN MORE

Grass Point

LOCH SPELVE

ARDMEANACH

Glen More

Ben Buie

Lochbuie

LOCH SCRIDAIN

Pennyghael

Moy Castle

LOCH BUIE

IONA

Ardtun

Carsaig

Fionnphort

Bunessan

ROSS OF MULL

Erraid

Uisken

0 1 2 3 5 6 7 8 9 10
Scale: Miles

THE ISLE OF
MULL

By the same author, in this series
The Island of Staffa

British Library
Cataloguing-in-Publication data.
A catalogue record for this book is available
from the British Library.

ISBN O 9521517 1 5
©Alastair de Watteville 1994

Published by:
Romsey Fine Art
PO Box 28, Romsey
Hampshire S051 OZF

Designed by:
David Trotman and Michael Goddard
Produced by: Graphics Ad Lib
Romsey, Hampshire

Photographs:
Dennis Bright: 16, 17, 24, 70, 71.
Burn Stewart plc: 48.
Edinburgh Photographic Library: 8, 9, 12,
13, 18, 31, 46, 47, 50, 54.
Graham Ellis: 53.
John Groom: 61.
David Howitt: 33, 52.
GrahamLangmuir: 39, 52.
The National Portrait Gallery: 11, 63.
The National Trust for Scotland: 22, 23, 34,
36, 37, 39, 67.
The Royal Commission for Ancient and
Historic Monuments of Scotland: 41, 42,
44, 49, 63, 64, 71.
Still Moving Picture Company: Front cover
and title page, 12, 20, 29, 40, 42, 44, 53, 54,
56, 57, 60, 70, 71, back cover.
Survival Anglia Limited: 14, 15.
Ronald Toms: Front cover inset, 9, 16, 18,
24, 26, 30, 31, 40, 44, 46, 48, 49, 51, 60.
Frank Walton: 65.
Estlin Waters: 24, 70, 71.
Frank Williams: 33.
Jack Williams: 31.
Other photographs: Alastair de Watteville.

Front cover: Ben More.
Front cover inset: Tobermory waterfront.
Title page: Duart Castle.
Back cover: Tobermory harbour sunrise.

THE ISLE OF

MULL

TRANQUILITY & SPECTACULAR BEAUTY IN THE INNER HEBRIDES

Alastair de Watteville

ROMSEY ℞ FINE ART

THE MAGIC OF MULL

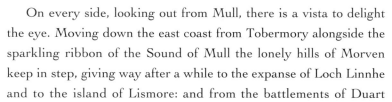

Waterfall between Torloisk and
Ulva Ferry.

What is it about Mull that appeals to you so much? The question evokes many different answers - different, but nearly always enthusiastic. For each of us, amongst the island's many attributes there is a great deal we find entrancing.

The jagged and varied coastline, the array of inviting islets, the distinctive maritime skyscapes, the colourful hills, the prolific wildlife, and the clean air delight the visitor: and the convenient ferry services, the high quality of local products, some first-rate hotels and restaurants, and the absence of crime provide the practical ingredients of a splendid holiday.

There is also a fascinating historical dimension. Everywhere on Mull there is evidence of the island's past. Some of it, such as the abandoned and ruined villages, is uncomfortable; some, including the castles and memorials, and the prehistoric forts, is stirring: all of it excites interest.

On every side, looking out from Mull, there is a vista to delight the eye. Moving down the east coast from Tobermory alongside the sparkling ribbon of the Sound of Mull the lonely hills of Morven keep in step, giving way after a while to the expanse of Loch Linnhe and to the island of Lismore: and from the battlements of Duart Castle the mass of Ben Nevis is sometimes in sight.

Southwards there are many small islands, as well as Scarba and behind, the Paps of Jura; and slightly to the right, the island of Colonsay. From high ground on Mull, on a good day and especially in the morning, beyond Tiree the chain of the Outer Hebrides

Duart Castle and Ben More.

can be seen to the west. And, finally, to the north there are Ardnamurchan, whose tip is the most westerly point of mainland Britain; the islands of Coll, Muck and Canna; the hills of Rum; and, faintly, the Cuillins of Skye.

Left: The Glen More road, looking
towards Ben Talaidh.
Inset: Old bridge at the head of Loch
Scridain.

The mountainous area of central Mull, looking east from the summit of Ben More.

Back on Mull itself the network of roads and tracks makes every part of the island accessible, and exploring any area a pleasure. But it was not always so. Early visitors faced numerous problems, and were apt to be outspoken in their judgement of Mull. William Sacheverell MP, for example, writing in 1702, said that the country was like a 'wild desert' . In 1773, on their visit to the Hebrides, Dr Johnson commented to James Boswell that 'the country is very rough, and my horse is but little'. Indeed, before the nineteenth century there were neither roads nor bridges on the island, and all progress must have been arduous. Today, gratefully, we can savour the island's treasures in comfort.

James Boswell.

Dr. Samuel Johnson.

MULL
THE
ISLAND

The Isle of Mull is part of the former county of Argyll, within Argyll & Bute District, itself part of what has been Strathclyde Region. At its closest Mull is only two miles from the mainland, across the Sound of Mull to Morven; and it is four miles from the island of Kerrera, off Oban. It lies at the southwestern end of the geological fault known as the Great Glen which runs across Scotland to Inverness.

Most people visiting Mull do so on the car ferry from Oban to Craignure, a distance of nine miles. There are two other crossings with timetabled sailings: Lochaline, in Morven, to Fishnish; and Kilchoan, in Ardnamurchan, to Tobermory. The road network, described later, in the section on the villages, is modest by some mainland standards. There is a programme of road improvement which residents are anxious to see implemented, especialy on the Tobermory - Salen section.

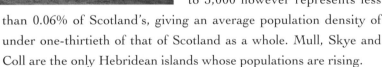

The Caledonian MacBrayne car ferry
'Isle of Mull' at Craignure.

In 1972 Loganair opened an air route to Mull from Glasgow, landing at Oban on the way; and in 1978 the company started flying to Mull direct from Glasgow. Soon afterwards, however, all scheduled flights were withdrawn, although the island's landing field at Glen Forsa near Salen has been kept open for private use.

Mull has an area of 346 square miles, or about 220,000 acres: that is some 2% of the total area of Scotland. The population of close to 3,000 however represents less

Grazing land near Ulva Ferry.

than 0.06% of Scotland's, giving an average population density of under one-thirtieth of that of Scotland as a whole. Mull, Skye and Coll are the only Hebridean islands whose populations are rising.

Almost three-quarters of the land is rough grazing, with just 3,500 acres of grassland and 250 acres under crops. There are about 40,000 acres of managed woodland, four-fifths of it belonging to Forest Enterprise. Although the island's mineral resources, particularly granite from Erraid and from just north of Fionnphort, and marble from Iona, were sold and exported in the past there is little which can be viably exploited now.

Left: Loch Scridain.
Inset: Ben More, seen across the mouth
of Loch na Keal.

He clasps the crag with
crooked hands;
Close to the sun in lonely
lands,
 Ring'd with the azure
world, he stands.
 The wrinkled sea beneath
him crawls;
 He watches from his
mountain walls,
 And like a thunderbolt he
falls.

Tennyson, The Eagle

Golden Eagle.

Two views of sunshine and shadow on the hills south-east of Ben More.

The distinctive scenery of Mull is almost wholly the result of intense volcanic activity roughly 50 million years ago. The deep lava flows which covered the underlying Moine Schists and Mesozoic sediments were subsequently attacked, and the appearance of the island modified, by the action of glaciers and running water. The mountainous area in the central eastern part of the island is composed of what remains of the ring dyke and caldera, and volcanic roots and cones, left behind by eruptions and gentler out-pourings over a lengthy period. Ben More which is in this jumbled zone has its summit at 3,169 feet: it is the highest top on Mull, and the only 'Munro' (3,000 foot mountain) on any of the Scottish islands apart from Skye. The plateaux formed by successive lava flows, known as *trap* country, exist in places on Mull, most notably on the Ardmeanach headland.

Golden Eagle.

South from Ardmeanach, across Loch Scridain, lies the Ross of Mull stretching towards Iona. The land gradually falls from the east towards Bunessan and Fionnphort to become rounded, with outcrops of pink granite holding pockets of peat, where the lava has been completely eroded away.

North of the isthmus between Gruline, at the head of Loch na Keal, and Salen, the scene is less rugged than in the central area. The terraced uplands and isolated flat hilltops mostly run down to tracts of moorland and marsh grass. This area includes Tobermory bay which is not only the best natural harbour in any of the islands but is also by far the most spectacular.

Buzzard, with food for chicks.

Thanks to its turbulent geological history, which gave rise to the heavily indented western coastline and to the rich variety of land types, and because of its range of weather patterns, Mull offers wildlife many kinds of habitats. The high ground provides rock, scree, short heather, and hill grasses: lower down, where severe or prolonged frosts are rare, there are woodlands, scrub, moor, grassland and bog; and bracken is plentiful. Around the coast and offshore there are cliffs, rocky and shingly beaches, and many islets and skerries.

Otter.

The Bearnach Burn joining the Lussa River close to Loch Spelve.

The island's prolific wildlife can be enjoyed in every month of the year.

There are red deer, hares, rabbits, stoats, polecats, weasels, and otters; and at sea, close by, there are often seals, basking sharks, dolphins, porpoises, and small whales. About 750 grey seal pups are born on the Treshnish Isles each autumn, and common seals breed on Mull itself. Everywhere there are birds; and Mull is excellent for birdwatching at all times of the year. More than 200 species have been identified, their survival in many cases being aided by the absence of foxes.

Birds that favour the shore and the sea are mentioned in later pages. Those that can sometimes be seen inland on Mull, amongst about 70 species that breed on the island, include buzzard, golden eagle, ptarmigan, snipe, redstart, stonechat, wheatear, and hooded crow. The white-tailed eagle, Europe's largest eagle which is regaining its foothold in the Inner Hebrides, is seen increasingly often on Mull.

Hooded Crow.

Redstart.

Ptarmigan.

Stonechat.

THE SHORE

Like the interior of the island, the form of the coastline is mainly determined by the flows of tertiary lava which once covered Mull and surrounding areas to a depth of several thousand feet. There is however rich variation: in a number of places the basalt has been completely eroded to reveal the underlying rock, as on the

The author's house on Loch na Keal.

western end of the Ross of Mull, and at some small unrelated sites round the coast; in others the erosion has created convoluted bays and headlands; and in a few, notably on Ulva and near Carsaig and around the Ardmeanach peninsula, hexagonal jointing akin to that on Staffa has been formed. Vertical movement of the island in relation to sea-level, both before and since the last ice age, has built raised beaches and shelves at heights of up to 160 feet above the current high-tide mark.

The long coast on the landward side of Mull, facing Morven across the Sound of Mull, is relatively unbroken, much of it forming the flanks of Salen Bay. In contrast, the western edge is heavily indented, with numerous small islands and skerries.

There are two principal sea lochs on this west coast, separated by the Ardmeanach peninsula; the more northerly of these inlets, Loch na Keal, which almost severs the north-western promontory of Mull from the rest; and Loch Scridain. Because it is hidden by the hills to the south and east, and because the sea bed can safely hold large vessels at anchor, the British Grand Fleet used to conceal warships in Loch na Keal during the Great War: and in the 1939-45 war the loch

A still October day on Loch na Keal.

was used as an assembly point for convoys about to cross the Atlantic. Loch Scridain also provides shelter, though for smaller craft; and additionally it gives fine panoramic views of the high ground of central Mull.

Left: The Clyde puffer 'Marsa' grounded by the falling tide in the Sound of Mull, ready to discharge cargo directly into vehicles brought alongside – a procedure which prompted the name of the restaurant in Salen.

Calgary beach, an arc of glistening pale sand, backed by machair, or flat grassland, with a curtain of trees and cliffs behind. Calgary in Alberta was named after this delightful spot. Another attractive, but less accessible, sandy beach is at Uisken, across the Ross from Bunessan.

The cliffs and steep slopes around the western tip of Ardmeanach contain an area known as *The Wilderness*, now belonging to the National Trust for Scotland. In a recess in the cliff face, a little above sea-level, is MacCulloch's Tree - the imprint of a 40-foot tall coniferous tree, preserved in the rock for over 50 million years, which is also an NTS property.

In the Ardmeanach cliff facing north-west towards Ulva there are several caves. One, Mackinnon's Cave, is large, exciting, and well-known as host to eerie legends: this cave is about 100 feet high and 40 feet wide at the entrance, tapering through intermediate caverns to a pitch-black chamber far inside the hill. Although the mouth of the cave is cut off by the sea at about half-tide, its floor is clean dry sand.

Across Loch Scridain near Bunessan there is a feature known as the Ardtun Leaf Beds. Here leaves and flowers have been preserved as fossils, caught in mud as they fell, and held prisoner by the layers of lava which flowed over them but which are now largely eroded.

On the south shore of the Ross of Mull steep cliffs run westwards from Carsaig, round Malcolm's Point, and on for a further four miles, with several streams tumbling down from the flatter ground above. Two miles along this cliff wall, by a re-entrant called the Nuns' Pass, is the Nuns' Cave, about 100 feet deep, formed when the level of the sea was higher than it is now. The cave contains on its west wall carvings of religious symbols, some possibly dating from the sixth century. It is said that nuns from Iona took refuge in the cave at the time of the Reformation.

Two miles along, the sea has made breaches in the cliff face to create weird shapes including openings called the Carsaig Arches.

Hexagonally-jointed basalt at the foot of the Burgh cliffs.

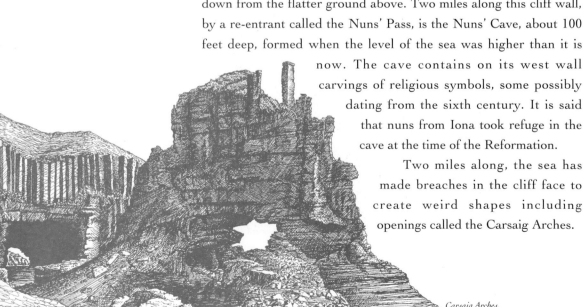

Carsaig Arches.

The Burgh, at the western extremity of the Ardmeanach headland.

MacCulloch's Tree. The standing
figure gives it scale.

The entrance to Mackinnon's Cave,
about 50 feet high.

Beside Loch Caol, Ardfenaig, near Bunessan.

Arctic Tern.

Part of the rock forming these cliffs is suitable for building and, in the 18th and 19th centuries, was quarried, particularly for use on Iona.

There are caves on Mull's north-west shore.

Ringed Plover.

Some, mainly in the Dervaig and Torloisk areas, are believed to have been used as illicit stills, making good quality spirit until the law was tightened up in about 1820. In this area, too, round one bend in the twisting road Calgary beach, with its surprising spread of silver sand, suddenly appears.

The lengthy foreshore takes many forms. There are cliffs, boulders of all sizes, shingle, and sand; and usually there are grassy banks or terraces behind and, in places, trees. Though the coastal rock is predominantly basalt, there are examples of granite, schist, sandstone, gneiss, and limestone. These materials give rise to conditions in which many species of birds are able to feed, and in some cases breed, not far from the water's edge: amongst the breeders are grey heron, mallard, eider, red-breasted merganser, oystercatcher, curlew, common sandpiper, black guillemot, and gulls and terns.

Oystercatcher.

Tidal streams do not exceed one knot, even at spring tides,

except off Duart Point, Caliach Point and in the Sound of Iona; the range is no more than 14 feet: there is thus scope for many kinds of activity around the shore. Commercial fishing, salmon and oyster farming, diving for crayfish, working lobster creels, and gathering whelks and mussels, all take place around Mull's coasts except when the weather makes this work dangerous or too difficult. In summer there are also leisure pursuits on the inshore waters: yachting, dinghy-sailing, sea-angling, sightseeing and birdwatching by boat.

Left: Grey Heron.
Over: Rocky shore, Loch Scridain, at low water.

LIFE ON MULL TODAY

Ferries bring 600,000 people, 125,000 cars and 4,000 coaches to Mull each year. Some of the people are island residents returning from trips to the mainland, but the great majority are visitors on holiday. Miraculously, Mull is not much disfigured by this annual invasion, half of which occurs in the eight weeks between mid-July and mid-September. One can only be astonished, as well as glad, that the normal life of the island goes on underneath the influx, and that it resurfaces unharmed as the numbers of visitors dwindle in the autumn: and that even at the height of the season the Mull countryside presents its usual calm and spacious aspect.

The pressure from so many people descending on the island is less than it might be because about 40 % of them are on one-day excursions, nearly all to Iona. These visitors board coaches at the Craignure ferry terminal and are taken straight to Fionnphort: there they use the local ferry to carry them to Iona where they are free to spend some hours before returning to Craignure.

Mull's hotels, guest houses, bed-and-breakfast establishments, self-catering units, camping grounds, and restaurants serve the remainder, who do stop on Mull: and they do so with remarkable elasticity, and in a most competent and unobtrusive way.

The revenue derived from tourism is important to Mull in providing financial stability and jobs. The island's other main sources of income are from the exports of agricultural and forestry products, and from social security payments. These payments are especially significant because the proportions of residents who are either above retirement age, or who are without employment, particularly in winter, are markedly above national averages.

Timber stacked near Craignure.

Agricultural and estate work occupy more of the working population than any other activity. Forestry, a major business producing 15,000 cubic metres of timber a year, used to be included in this group but it no longer furnishes more than a few jobs as nearly all Forest Enterprise work is now placed with contractors based off Mull.

Inset above left:
Fisherman at Tobermory.
Right: A Mull fishing boat at the
Fionnphort slipway.

Fisherman attending to his catch, at Tobermory.

Cross-bred Highland cattle are seen more frequently than in the past.

Sheep down from the hill.

There are about 140 farms and 85 crofts on Mull. These crofts, predominantly on the Ross, but also near Dervaig and Salen, are properties protected by successive Acts of Parliament. More than half the total agricultural area is owner-occupied. The nature and extent of the ground, and the policy on subsidies and support prices, have led to an emphasis on sheep which do well on the hill land even though each one needs on average three acres of rough grazing. There are about 60,000 sheep, half of them breeding ewes; and 3,000 to 4,000 cattle, mostly suckled beef calves and yearling store animals. There is a modest but growing dairy and milk distribution business. A few farmers keep pigs on a small scale. Nursery gardening is carried on in the north of the island.

Traditional sheep-shearing near Bunessan.

Retailing locally woven products.

A formidable difficulty facing all farmers is the distance to markets. Fleeces have virtually no value: but stock, at best, has to go to Oban; more often it has to be conveyed to Dalmally or even to Perth or Stirling for sale.

There are fishing fleets at Tobermory and Bunessan, and lone commercial fishermen with their own vessels at other points on the coast. Catches, again, have long journeys to market. Fish and oyster farming and fish processing are well established.

The service sector offers a number of jobs, some of them seasonal and some which can be shared. Both categories include work in the accommodation, catering and leisure fields. About a quarter of the active working-age population is engaged in some kind of self-employed endeavour. The list of ventures, all of which offer attractive products or services, includes summer painting schools at Carsaig and Calgary, weaving, jewellery design and manufacture, silverwork, metal sculpture, pottery, soft toy construction, chocolate-making and crook-making.

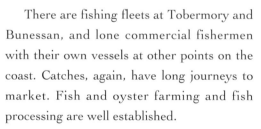
Fish farm, Loch Spelve.

Mull potter and silversmith at work.

Recreational pursuits for visitors are plentiful. They include magnificent walking, for which maps and guide books are on sale in the shops. There is golf at Tobermory and Craignure; and sea-angling, sailing and boating at Tobermory and at other places on the coast. Mull is able to provide bird-watchers with great opportunities for spotting species seldom or never seen on the mainland. For the geologist, historian, and archaeologist there is generous scope for research. There is good fresh water fishing: for salmon in the River Ba and Loch Ba, in the Lussa river which flows into Loch Spelve and, possibly, in Loch Frisa; and for brown or rainbow trout in Loch

The Regatta fleet under spinnaker in the Sound of Mull.

Frisa, Loch Torr and the Mishnish lochs. Stalking can sometimes be arranged. Information is widely available on how to obtain licences, where they are needed, and on making bookings.

Housing on Mull is a topic of frequent debate because of the unusual pattern of tenure. Of the stock of about 1,300 dwellings, nearly a fifth, 250, are second homes or holiday homes. Many residents feel that this proportion is already too high, and that any increase in it would be bound to threaten the nature of island society. Of the balance, less than half is owner-occupied and more than half is rented.

Schooling is adapted to the geography of Mull. There are dispersed primary schools, some of them very small, and a well-regarded secondary school in Tobermory which was expanded in the 1980s to enable pupils to take their Scottish Certificate of Education 'Highers' there.

Generally, the arrangements made for living on the island allow residents to do so in a civilised and comfortable way. There is a church, kirk or chapel for each main denomination; health services; 120 miles of road, mostly rather narrow but with enough passing places; modern telephone connections; good TV reception; a mobile bank; a travelling library; electricity almost everywhere; and piped water in the villages and settlements.

Mull's calendar contains a number of events which are peculiar to Mull, including the Highland Games at Tobermory, the Salen Show, and the West Highland Regatta which ends at Tobermory. Late in May there is the air rally at the Glen Forsa airfield, two miles east of Salen, at which machines long out of regular service assemble to provide a colourful and nostalgic pageant.

The airfield at Glen Forsa during the annual air rally.

In mid-October there is the Tour of Mull car rally. This is a competition in the RAC calendar, spread over three days and always attracting the maximum permitted number of entrants. For a week Mull becomes alive with the support teams and their workshop vehicles, mountains of spare tyres, scrutineering bays and all the paraphernalia of motor sport. The conduct of the rally, governed by Strathclyde Regional Council regulations, includes the closing of certain roads for five hours. The day before the start of the rally farmers take care to move their stock into byres or at least well clear of the road; and spectators are similarly ushered into approved areas.

Taking a watersplash at speed during the Tour of Mull car rally.

Another competitor in a hurry.

A rally participant.

These events are interesting and well-attended, and they go some way to spreading the months over which visitors come to the island, for their own benefit and for the benefit of residents.

People living on Mull in the 19th century and in the first three-quarters of the 20th century endured a fall in their numbers of more than 80%. Between 1820 and 1970 the population fell from about 10,600 to about 2,100. The 1981 census was the first for over 150 years to reveal any growth.

LIFE ON MULL YESTERDAY

There were several interlinked factors which together brought about the collapse in numbers, though economics was always the ultimate determinant of what happened. During the period of conflict in Europe from 1793 to 1815 there was relative prosperity on Mull: this was partly due to the return in the 1780s of soldiers from the American War of Independence, bringing money, for a few years a supply of labour, and, soon, an increase in the birth-rate; but more importantly it was due to a halting of the supply of barilla from Spain.

Barilla is an impure alkali containing potash which was crucial as a fertiliser at that time. It grew vigorously around the shores of Spain, and was imported into Britain. When the barilla trade was interrupted by war the use of *kelp* was substituted. This consisted of the ash of *laminaria* seaweed (now itself called kelp) which is similarly rich in potash and which is found plentifully around Mull and Ulva. Kelp sales rose from 100 tons at £3 a ton in the 1760s to 600 tons at £20 a ton by 1815, only to fall again to £3 a ton by 1834 when the import of barilla, duty-free, had become re-established.

During the years of plenty the population continued to rise; and it went on doing so for some years afterwards, helped by the return of about 1,000 officers and men at the end of the Napoleonic Wars in 1815, and also by improved medical care including the introduction of vaccine against smallpox. The number of crofts grew in step with the population, although because of increasing congestion many of the new ones were too small to be economically viable except in the most favourable conditions. Lairds, however, became accustomed to a more comfortable life-style.

Above left: A well-known figure on the Ross of Mull between the wars, beside his lobster boat.

Harvesting at Burg Farm, Ardmeanach, in the 1920s.

Cottage at Kintra.

A thatched byre, near Fionnphort.

At a period when practically everyone was engaged in agriculture these landowners needed rents from all their crofts to maintain their estates. But where the crofts were too small to generate the required rent purely from their parcels of land, the crofters were forced to rely additionally on fishing and kelp production. When the kelp market almost disappeared, and by chance at the same time cod and herring largely deserted Mull's sea lochs, the crofters very soon became unable to pay their rents.

Landowners reacted quickly to the drop in their incomes. By forcibly removing crofters from their homes, in a process known as the Clearances, they were able to run sheep on the land. This was at once more cost-effective than using it for crofting, especially as successful Lowland sheep farmers were at that time looking for extra land to graze, and were offering good payment for the use of ground on Mull. A further reduction in the population was caused by some people, fearing eviction, moving out voluntarily: to search for jobs, hard or impossible to find on the islands; or to respond to the lure of new lives elsewhere especially in Canada, Australia and New Zealand.

Family outside their home, Ardmeanach, 1901.

The severe hardship caused to many families by this upheaval was gravely exacerbated by the potato blight, *Phytophthora Infestans*, which had devastated Ireland and which spread to Mull in 1845. Potatoes had been introduced to Mull in the closing years of the 18th century, and by

In 1750 this huge boulder broke off the Gribun cliffs and fell, obliterating the cottage in which John and Rachel Macfadyen were spending their wedding night.

1820 because of their many advantages they accounted for four-fifths of the islanders' nourishment.

An abandoned croft near Ulva Ferry.

The tragedy brought about by the destruction within a few months of every potato crop on the island can scarcely be imagined: it added urgent impetus to the desire of many to emigrate; but nonetheless hundreds starved.

To believe that these horrors were brought about just by the actions of rapacious lairds would be a mistake. Many made strenuous efforts to help their tenants in a number of ways including the payment of their fares to the colonies; and as reports of the hardships reached Edinburgh and London government schemes aimed at relieving the worst distress were gradually adopted, though the physical isolation of Mull from the mainland made remedial measures less effective than they might have been.

On the road to Burg Farm, 1901.

Before marine engines came into use the principal crossing from Oban to Mull made its landfall at Grass Point. This route had been used ever since people first lived on Mull for passengers and produce, and for taking stock to market in Oban, sometimes by way of Kerrera to reduce the open sea passage to under four miles. Drove roads across Mull, which were followed by animals from Tiree and Coll usually put ashore at Croig, as well as those originating on Mull, converged on Grass Point.

Paddle-steamer leaving Salen pier on her way to Tobermory, about 1930.

In 1880 the railway linking Oban to Callander and Glasgow was completed. At once there was a surge in demand for journeys to Mull from travellers starting as far away as the Lowlands. The paddle-steamer *Pioneer* in 1881 became the first regular ferry on the Oban - Mull run; then from 1893 until 1908 the larger *Carabineer*, another paddle-steamer, took over; she was followed by the *Grenadier*, and then by the *Lochinvar* which operated continuously until 1955 . Throughout this period cruising round Mull became popular. From 1936 to 1974 the stately MacBrayne turbine steamer *King George V* made these cruises daily in summer.

Until 1964, most people going to Mull landed at Tobermory after following a zig-zag course to Craignure, Lochaline in Morven, Salen, Drimnin in Morven, and finally reaching Tobermory some three and a half hours after leaving Oban. Passengers wishing to disembark at Craignure were taken ashore by lighter. Any vehicle to be conveyed to Mull was carried as deck cargo, discharged at Tobermory either by crane or by driving over two planks spanning the gap to the pier, depending on the state of the tide.

M. V. Lochinvar at Tobermory's new pier, 1954.

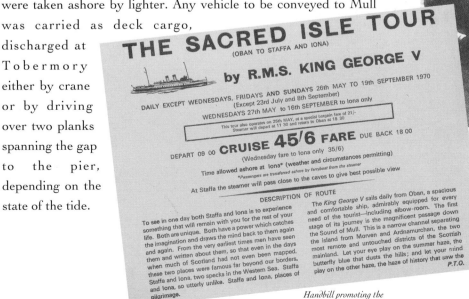

THE SACRED ISLE TOUR
(OBAN TO STAFFA AND IONA)
by R.M.S. KING GEORGE V

DAILY EXCEPT WEDNESDAYS, FRIDAYS AND SUNDAYS 26th MAY TO 19th SEPTEMBER 1970
(Except 23rd July and 8th September)
WEDNESDAYS 27th MAY to 16th SEPTEMBER to Iona only

This tour also operates on 25th MAY, at a special bargain fare of 21/-
Steamer will depart at 11 30 and return to Oban at 18 30

DEPART 09 00 CRUISE **45/6** FARE DUE BACK 18 00
(Wednesday fare to Iona only 35/6)

Time allowed ashore at Iona* (weather and circumstances permitting)
*Passengers are transferred ashore by ferryboat from the steamer
At Staffa the steamer will pass close to the caves to give best possible view

DESCRIPTION OF ROUTE

To see in one day both Staffa and Iona is to experience something that will remain with you for the rest of your life. Both are unique. Both have a power which catches the imagination and draws the mind back to them again and again. From the very earliest times men have seen them and written about them, so that even in the days when much of Scotland had not even been mapped, these two places were famous far beyond our borders. Staffa and Iona, two specks in the Western Sea. Staffa and Iona, so utterly unlike. Staffa and Iona, places of pilgrimage.

The *King George V* sails daily from Oban, a spacious and comfortable ship, admirably equipped for every need of the tourist—including elbow-room. The first stage of its journey is the magnificent passage down the Sound of Mull. This is a narrow channel separating the island from Morven and Ardnamurchan, the two most remote and untouched districts of the Scottish mainland. Let your eye play on the summer haze, the butterfly blue that dusts the hills; and let your mind play on the other haze, the haze of history that saw the
P.T.O.

Handbill promoting the round-Mull cruise in 1970.

In 1964 the new pier at Craignure was completed, and it immediately became the main arrival point on Mull for passengers and vehicles from Oban. The first ship to work this route was *Columba* which had an internal car-deck, with a hoist for bringing vehicles up to the top deck for discharge across a ramp on to the pier. In 1976 the roll-on/roll-off ferry *Caledonia* took over the run; and she in turn gave way to *Isle of Mull* in 1988.

For much of the l9th century Mull lagged behind almost every other area in the provision of roads. One effect was that people continued longer than elsewhere to provide themselves with most of what they required: clothing from their own sheep, leather from their own cattle, food from their land. Until almost the end of the century the small amount of mail reaching Mull was distributed on foot by the postman.

Improvements in the ferry services gave a spur to the improvement of the island's roads, and thereby to the more efficient provision of services including health care and schooling, and for the distribution of goods of all kinds, though the supply of electricity across Mull was completed only in the 1970s, and the introduction of refuse collection came even later.

Under the Education Act of 1872 the State took over control of all schools: lessons were to be delivered in English not Gaelic, attendance to age thirteen became compulsory, and secondary schools were established. On Mull the primary schools beside the roads, and the secondary school in Tobermory, date from this Act. The illiteracy level of about 25% at that time was fairly quickly eradicated. The tide of emigration which ran into the 20th century was latterly due not to the actions of landowners but to the choice

Sheep-shearing at Tiroran, Mull, 1916.

of young people whose ambitions had been stimulated by their education. Mull is too small to hold all the trained and talented people it produces, and it accepts that some will go across the sea to thrive.

MONUMENTS FORTS & CASTLES

Mull abounds with monuments, some dating from 2,000 BC, early in the bronze age. There are standing stones in many parts of the island, clustered particularly north and west of Dervaig, near Gruline and at the western end of the Ross. Some, perhaps most, of the stones formed parts of stone circles; but the only complete circles left are at Lochbuie where there are two close to each other. There are also two cup-marked stones from the same period near Calgary bay. Burial chambers, known as *cists*, have come to light in the Gruline and Salen area.

Bronze age food vessels and beakers have been found at Salen and in Quinish. Iron age presence on Mull has left its mark conspicuously in the form of circular forts, or *duns*. All are in ruins. The most impressive is Dun Aisgean near the shore two miles north of Gometra, across Loch Tuath. Another is Dun Urgadul about a mile out of Tobermory on the Glengorm road; and a third is Dun nan Gall half way between Ulva Ferry and Torloisk.

More recent monuments include that to Dougal MacPhail, composer of the Mull anthem *At t'Eilean Muileach* and sometimes called the Bard of Mull, which stands beside the road through Glen More at the junction by Loch Spelve. Further along the same road going towards Bunessan, half a mile past Pennyghael, stands the Beaton Cairn. It is in fact a stone cross on a stepped base, carrying the date 1582, erected in memory of a family of Mull doctors who for generations practiced medicine with remarkable skill not just on Mull but throughout the Hebrides, and one of whom was given the title 'Chief Physician of the Isles' by King James VI.

Three miles east of Salen, by the graveyard which is still in use, there is what remains of a 14th century chapel called Pennygown. Two of the stone slabs are believed to be over the bodies of a 15th century Maclean chief and his wife.

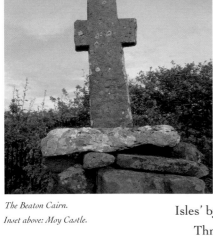

The Beaton Cairn.
Inset above: Moy Castle.

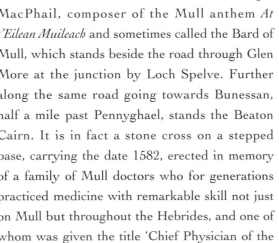

Aros Castle from the south.

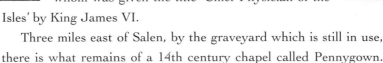

Aros Castle from the north-west.

The monument to Dougal MacPhail.

Aros Castle

*Dun Aisgean: The ruins of an early
circular fortification, 35 feet in
diameter, overlooking Loch Tuath.*

There are three medieval castles on Mull that are readily accessible, and one other in ruins five miles west-north-west of Tobermory called Dun Ara.

Aros Castle two miles north of Salen is also ruined; but when it was built in the 14th century, and for the following three hundred years, it was a structure of notable strength and importance. The thickness of its walls, still evident despite their condition, suggests a keep that the builders intended to be impregnable. It was a stronghold of the Lords of the Isles throughout this period until their power ended with the Highlanders' defeat at Culloden. The castle occupies a site with commanding views over the Sound of Mull and Salen Bay, and is protected on the seaward side by cliffs.

Duart Castle

Duart Castle standing on Duart Point three miles south-east of Craignure, is largely open to the public. It dates from the 13th century, and for a long time was the home of the Chief of Clan Maclean. In 1692 the clan lost the castle to the Campbells, who allowed it to become dilapidated. Sir Fitzroy Maclean, then chief of the clan, bought Duart back for the Macleans in 1912 and immediately restored it with great ingenuity, preserving most of what had previously existed while making it meet the standards of building of the 20th century.

Paul Sandby's sketch of Duart Castle, 1748.

Subsequently exhibitions, including a presentation of scouting worldwide, and a tableau in the dungeons, have been added. The castle has a powerful position, dominating the Sound of Mull, Loch Linnhe and the Firth of Lorne.

Duart Castle from the south-west.

Moy Castle and Lochbuie House.

Torosay Castle.   *Statue in Torosay Castle grounds.*

*An axonometric drawing of
Moy Castle from the north.*

Moy Castle

Moy Castle stands on a low rock platform at the head of Loch Buie. It is a modest-sized tower house dating from the 15th century, occupied until 1750 by the MacLaines of Lochbuie. It incorporates three main floors, with additions, all in a fair state of preservation; but entry is forbidden because of the uncertain condition of the stonework.

Glengorm Castle.

There are two substantial Victorian piles, Glengorm and Torosay, which were designed for residential as opposed to defensive purposes.

Glengorm Castle

Glengorm Castle was erected in 1860. It is a fine symmetrical building with extensive views to Ardnamurchan and the islands to the north. The estate was used as a sporting base in the latter part of the l9th century: it is privately owned, and its current activities include market gardening, furnishing all Mull with vegetables.

Torosay Castle

Torosay Castle, a mile south-east of Craignure, was built in 1856. It has a fine interior which embodies lavish features of the Scottish baronial style. The grounds which look out over Duart Bay are laid out to a design by Sir John Lorimer as an Italian garden, with terraces, balustrades and statues, and some handsome trees. In 1950 the property was offered for sale as a 'comfortable modernised castle at present run as a hotel'. It is now open to the public each year until mid-October.

TOBERMORY

Tobermory waterfront and piers.

The name Tobermory came readily from the Gaelic *Tobar Mhoire*, Mary's Well. Above the town in the cemetery there are the foundations of the ancient Chapel of St Mary, and nearby, across the road, is the site of the well itself.

Tobermory bay from above the town.

Since the middle of the 19th century Tobermory has been home to about one-third of the population of Mull. Now that the island's numbers are growing again that proportion is likely to increase because most of the growth is taking place in and around Tobermory. It is

Fishing craft at the old pier.

very much the capital of Mull, formally a burgh with local government and central government offices, the large parish church, the High School, the church on Main Street now called The Gallery which is a focus for Mull crafts, the Aros Hall lecture and social centre, the bank, fire service, museum, tourist information office, hotels and restaurants, and many other amenities.

Piped water was provided in Tobermory in 1882, electricity in 1926, and a telephone service in 1931. Although the town was not exactly leading the world with these utilities, installing them on Mull required skill and determination; and they transformed the lives of those within reach of them.

Rubha nan Gall lighthouse a mile north of Tobermory.

Before 1788 few people lived down by the sea where the present town is, preferring to be on the higher pasture and grazing land behind, to derive a livlihood from animals and grain. Then in that year the Scottish Fishery Board, an agency of the British Society for Extending Fisheries, made Tobermory into a new fishing village; but it only partially fulfilled the ambitions of the planners because there were not enough fish, and competition from Oban was too intense.

Today's waterfront dates from that time. It is built on a strip of land reclaimed from the harbour, and held in place by a sea wall. Thomas Telford advised on the design of the wall, and on the materials to be used, in 1790. The construction of the 'old pier' in 1835 in the centre of the town followed his principles. There are two other piers: the Caledonian MacBrayne pier, or 'new pier', built to the north of the old pier in 1864 by the proprietor of the Mishnish estates, and extended in 1930 and further modified in 1985; and the pier by the distillery.

Tobermory's Ledaig Distillery was opened in 1798, and its pier built in 1823. The site was chosen because the water in the Tobermory River, falling steeply from the moors, was judged to be ideal for a malt whisky; and could be channelled directly under the distillery building. After thirty-nine years the distillery closed, only to reopen in 1878, and to close again in 1928. In 1972 it reopened once more, but this time the business lasted just three years. Now, happily, after restarting production, *Tobermory* single malt is yet again being supplied to bars and shops over a wide area.

As well as presenting a scene of great beauty, Tobermory bay has the virtues of an excellent anchorage. When the Spannish Armada was driven up the east side of England to become scattered as it made its way round the north of Scotland and then southwards on the long run back to Spain, many of its ships were lost. One Armada vessel, long thought to be the galleon *Florencia*, or *Florida*, carrying the pay for the army, somehow found and took shelter in the bay in September, 1588; then, according to legend, as she was later preparing to set sail having carried out essential repairs she exploded and sank a few yards from what is now the site of the new pier. Strenuous effort have been made, off and on, over four hundred years to recover priceless

An aerial view of the town taken in 1978.

treasure from the harbour floor: not much has been retrieved; but just enough to keep the appetite for renewed exploration whetted. Now the vessel is believed to have been not a man-of-war but a Mediterranean carrack called *San Juan de Sicilia* which had been carrying soldiers, but no cash. A section of the Mull Museum in Tobermory is devoted to the story of the Armada ship.

Sunrise, Tobermory bay.

The principal roads of Mull form a figure-of-8, with a tail out to the west from the lower, or southern, loop. These roads link the villages to each other, to the various settlements, and to Tobermory. Dervaig is on the upper, or northern, loop; Salen is at the point where the loops meet; Craignure is on the lower loop; and Bunessan, and Fionnphort, lie on the tail.

FIVE VILLAGES

Dervaig

Dervaig was designed and built in 1799 by Maclean of Coll as 26 houses arranged in pairs, each with its own plot of land and direct access to the common hill grazing. The parish church by the village crossroads, which dates from a hundred years later, is a landmark: it has good glass, and is notable for its distinctive pencil-shaped spire.

Tobermory to Dervaig is a twisting seven miles. Two miles on there is a turning to the tiny port of Croig, and a further 24 miles brings the traveller to Salen by way of Calgary. Alternatively, by taking the road over the moor to Torloisk a few miles can be saved, at the expense of missing some of the finest views in the Hebrides.

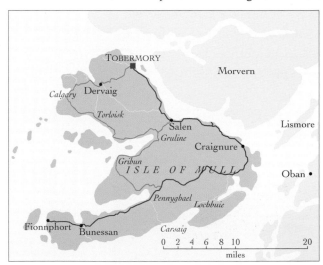

On this route, about a mile out of Dervaig, there is a novel and informative presentation of Mull history which includes a *black house* and a *white house* from the 19th century, bringing back the lifestyle, dress and diet of those days, and an exhibition of the island's plants and animals.

Beside the church there is turning which offers a different way to Salen, down the 'glen road'. On the left after a few hundred yards is the Mull Little Theatre, Britain's smallest professional theatre, built in a stone barn, with seating for 40. The glen road joins the Tobermory - Salen road at Aros Bridge, two miles north of Salen.

Dervaig from the Tobermory road. The village is largely hidden by the bracken-covered ridge.

Salen

Like Dervaig, Salen was deliberately planned and built. In the 18th century a few families had clustered on the flat and relatively fertile isthmus between Salen Bay and Gruline. Then in 1800 General Macquarie, who is mentioned in the paragraphs about Ulva, built the present village which has changed little since then. The name Jarvisfield on Macquarie's memorial tablet in the mausoleum at Gruline refers to the area he owned, which included Salen.

St Columba is said to have spoken at Salen; and the stream running north into the village is called *The Burn of the Sermons* to commemorate his visits.

Every August the Salen Show,

Salen Bay.

which attracts exhibitors and visitors from considerable distances, takes place nearby. This event was first held in 1832 and is possibly the oldest agricultural show in the Highlands and Islands.

M. V. Lochinvar leaving Salen pier, 1935.

Before the modern pier at Craignure came into service Salen pier, now in ruins, was an important stop for vessels carrying passengers or freight along the Sound of Mull.

Craignure

The pier at Craignure is so busy in the summer that the village has a bustling and mildly frenzied air. The ground rises steeply behind the buildings, limiting the possibilities of relieving the congestion around the coaches, shops, stalls, and information centre by expansion away from the water's edge. On the flat promontory half a mile up the coast, however, a substantial hotel standing in wide, open grounds was opened in the early 1970s.

Craignure is almost as well known for its railway as for its pier. In June 1984 the only passenger railway ever to be built on any Scottish island went into service. The 10¼-inch gauge Mull Railway links the Craignure

The Mull Rail Station at Craignure.

The train making its way to Torosay Castle.

terminus, behind the old pier, with Torosay Castle, a mile down the line.

The Mull and West Highland Narrow Gauge Railway Company, to give its full name, has the trappings of any of its bigger mainland brothers - platforms, signals, turntables, and, of course, a ticket office. The two steam locomotives, and the one diesel, take turns at drawing the three carriages, complying with the published but delightfully relaxed timetable which accords with the tempo of island holidaying.

One of the steam locomotives on the turntable at the terminus.

Bunessan

On leaving Craignure, on the way to Bunessan, the road soon reverts to single track. It runs through wild Glen More, returning to the shore at the head of Loch Scridain. Here it is joined by the other road from Salen which followed the southern edge of Loch na Keal, passed under the Gribun cliffs, and cut across the Ardmeanach peninsula. After three miles, at Pennyghael, there is a turning to Carsaig. Bunessan lies nine miles further on.

Johnson and Boswell took this route beside the north shore of Loch Scridain, in the opposite direction, when they were returning from Iona, making their way to Lochbuie. Progress must have been slow and exhausting for them, as there was no road between Pennyghael and Bunessan then or, indeed, until 1855, eighty years later. Understandably, they broke their journey near Bunessan.

Fionnphort jetty, looking to Iona.

Fishing boats at Bunessan pier.

The present village is built as a crescent of white houses and shops, facing across the road to the water of Loch na Lathaich, a shallow inlet which provides fair shelter for fishing craft; and which receives occasional cargo ships at its pier half a mile west of the village. There is a lighthouse at the entrance to the bay to warn shipping of the hazardous shoals and rocks.

Inland from Bunessan, a little over a mile south-east across the moor, is Loch Assapol which is both the reservoir for the village and a source of brown and rainbow trout.

The house outside Bunessan where Johnson and Boswell broke their journey from Iona to Lochbuie in 1773.

The Tormore quarry in 1980.

Fionnphort

Once clear of Bunessan the nature of the scenery changes abruptly as the underlying pink granite emerges. Smoothly rounded rock outcrops are on all sides for the five miles to Fionnphort. The pale sand associated with this granite explains the name of the village which means fair haven. This is the end of the road on Mull, and the taking off place for Iona.

Fionnphort is the youngest of our five villages. It has become more established, and grown, as the passenger traffic to and from Iona has increased.

Half a mile north across the heather is the quarry of Tormore. Until about 1895 the quarry supplied building firms with granite blocks of the finest quality. The stone was largely free of flaws and grain, and would take intricate carving as well as a splendid polish. It was chosen for Blackfriars Bridge, Holborn Viaduct, the Albert Memorial, and for many other structures for which its special characteristics were wanted. The end must have come suddenly for the quarry:

granite awaiting shipment, and in every stage of preparation, was left near the jetty. However, renewed demand for the stone led to the issue, in 1989, of a licence to resume quarrying.

On the Mull side of the Sound of Iona, just a little past Tormore, is *Eilean nam Ban*, meaning the isle of women. When St Columba was in charge on Iona he was said to have had the island's women banished there, at least from time to time, because they were such a nuisance.

In addition to serving the Iona ferry, Fionnphort is also the road junction for the tiny port of Kintra two miles to the north and for the isle of Erraid to the south.

The Atlantic coast of Iona.

IONA

Sunset over Iona.
Inset above: Iona Abbey buildings from Iona Sound.

An Iona beach.

Iona is of such importance that it deserves a book to itself; and indeed much has been published about the island. Some of the material recorded elsewhere is naturally inconsistent between one source and another, but as the general thrust of the story is so majestic that hardly matters.

Stepping ashore on Iona is an experience virtually certain to delight each visitor. The visual impact of the place itself and the grand views of Mull and the nearby islands, overlaid with the historic and religious associations, affect everyone. Inevitably, because of Iona's widespread appeal, most visitors find themselves

The west door of the Cathedral, St. Martin's Cross and Abbey buildings.

there in the company of substantial numbers of others; but anyone able to stand or walk alone is likely to be even more entranced.

Over: The Cathedral and Abbey buildings from the north-west.

FIFTY EIGHT

Iona Abbey by William Daniell, 1817.

It seems certain that before St Columba landed on Iona in the year 563 , bringing Christianity to Scotland from Ireland, there had for a long time been devotional practices including sun-worship on the island. During the 34 years he lived on Iona, Columba built it into the base for his evangelical crusade throughout Europe. And the island was so revered as a holy place that more than 40 early Scottish kings lie buried there, and their memorials can be seen in the abbey museum.

Norse raiders assailed Iona at least six times in the eighth, ninth and tenth centuries, some of their atrocities being commemorated in the names of the places on the island where they occurred. Following the establishment of the Benedictine order in about 1200 , several fine stone ecclesiastical buildings were erected, including the nunnery whose attractive remains still stand today; and in 1500 the abbey was accorded cathedral status. But Iona's woes returned sixty years later in the Reformation when all the buildings were demolished, and all but three of the 350 stone crosses smashed: and historic documents taken from Iona for safety were later found and destroyed by Cromwell.

The east window of the Cathedral.

Dr Samuel Johnson's desire and determination to see Iona prompted his journey with James Boswell to the Western Isles of Scotland in 1773. Despite the total neglect in which they found what was left of the abbey buildings they were deeply moved by the island. Johnson expressed the emotion they experienced in his often-quoted observation: *That man is little to be envied, whose patriotism would not gain force upon the plain of Marathon, or whose piety would not grow warmer amongst the ruins of Iona.*

In 1899 The Duke of Argyll gave the ruined abbey buildings to the Church of Scotland. The cathedral was restored, and brought into use in 1910; and in 1938 Dr George MacLeod set up the Iona Community which immediately set about reconstructing the monastic buildings. The remainder of Iona was subsequently acquired by the National Trust for Scotland.

A similar view today.

Pebbles on an Iona beach.

Between Iona and Mull is the Sound of Iona, a stretch of very clear but sometimes turbulent water about a mile wide: and administratively too Iona is separate from Mull, each island having its own community council. Geologically the two islands are separate entities: the extreme eastern end of the Ross of Mull, where Fionnphort stands, is granite, whereas Iona is mostly made of Torridonian sandstone with gneiss and gravel on its western fringe. There is marble, which used to be quarried, in the south-east of the island; and marble pebbles are to be found on the sparkling white beaches.

Agriculture has been carried on successfully on Iona. In the first half of the nineteenth century, when Iona's population was 500, the island exported both grain and cattle. In tune with Mull and the Hebrides in general Iona's population dwindled in the succeeding hundred years falling to 60 in the 1940s. It now seems to have stabilised at between 120 and 140.

Only one of Mull's islands lies to the east. That is the mile-long fertile Calve Island which protects Tobermory Bay, allowing it to be such an attractive anchorage. All the rest are to the west. Ignoring the large number of reefs and skerries that lie off Mull, these islands are Erraid, Erisgeir, Inch Kenneth, Eorsa, Little Colonsay, Staffa, Ulva and Gometra, and the Treshnish Isles.

MULL'S OWN ISLANDS

They generally enjoy more sunshine and have less rain than Mull itself. With the exception of Inch Kenneth and parts of Erraid and Little Colonsay they are composed wholly of basalt. They all rise from a gently graded sea bed nowhere more than 50 metres deep between Mull and the islands, though 100 metres deep between Iona and the Treshnish Isles. The edge of the continental shelf is 120 miles out to the west.

Throughout these islands seabirds can be sen on their nests, on the wing, and swimming. They are most prolific, and most exciting, at Lunga in the Treshnish Isles.

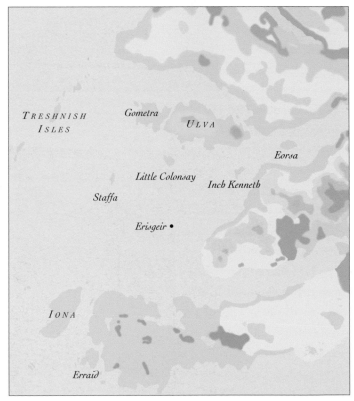

Inset: Iona seen from a bracken-covered hillside on Erraid.

Erraid

Off the south-western tip of the Ross of Mull lies the island of Erraid. For an hour or two either side of low water it is linked to the Ross by a broad expanse of sand.

The island measures about a mile in each direction. It is composed mainly of grey granite and largely covered with bracken. Exploration is heavy-going but the views of Iona, three miles away, and the nearby rocks and skerries are rewarding; and in wild conditions the roar of breakers is awesome.

The falling tide uncovering the strand linking Erraid to the Ross of Mull.

R obert Louis Stevenson, born in Edinburgh in 1850, was brought up on Erraid. His father practised as a structural engineer, and was engineer to the Board of Northern Lights. He quarried the island's granite for use in the construction of the lighthouses south of Tiree at Skerryvore and Dubh Artach, and also exported it for other builders. Late in the nineteenth century this trade came to an end as the handling and transport of Erraid granite became uneconomical.

Visitors to Erraid can see the disused quarry with the large mound of undressed granite blocks that never found buyers, and the stone cottages of the quarry workers.

In Stevenson's *Kidnapped* the hero, eighteen-year-old Davie Balfour, is shipwrecked and marooned on Erraid. Because he kept watch mainly to the west and north-west he did not realise for more than three days, during which time he almost starved, that he was on a half-tide island.

R. L. Stevenson. Painting by Sir William Blake Richmond, 1887.

Skerryvore lighthouse, south-west of Tiree, built of Erraid granite.

Quarried granite and a ruined quarryman's cottage on Erraid.

Inch Kenneth

I nch Kenneth is a low, wedge-shaped island, a mile long and up to half a mile wide, lying almost a mile off the Mull coast at Gribun. It is named after Kenneth, one of St Columba's followers who accompanied him from Ireland.

Unlike the rest of Mull and its islands Inch Kenneth is formed of limestone. The soil is exceptionally fertile, having at times supported a population of 100 on its 130 acres, thanks to the ability to grow robust crops of oats, barley and potatoes, and to feed cattle and sheep.

There is a ruined chapel on Inch Kenneth, and an aged graveyard holding the remains of chieftains and other distinguished leaders. The island was often chosen as a resting place by pilgrims on their way to Iona, and is said to have once had a seminary for training eccliastics.

Johnson and Boswell spent two days on Inch Kenneth in 1773 as the guests of Sir Allan Maclean, chief of the clan. At that time the only people living on the island were Sir Allan, his two daughters, and their servants. Johnson was captivated by his visit, and wrote:

. . .occupied not by a gross herdsman, or amphibious fisherman, but by a gentleman and two ladies, of high birth, polished manners, and elegant conversation, who, in a habitation raised not very far above the ground, but furnished with unexpected neatness and convenience, practised all the kindness of hospitality, and refinement of courtesy.

In 1933 the family that had owned Inch Kenneth for the previous ten years sold it to Sir Harold Boulton, the writer and editor of three volumes of Scottish songs and writer of *The Skye Boat Song*.

Five years later the island was bought by David Mitford, 2nd Lord Redesdale, and Lady Redesdale, as a home for themselves, their son Thomas and their daughters Nancy, Pamela, Diana, Unity, Jessica, and Deborah. Lord Redesdale died in 1958, and Lady Redesdale died on Inch Kenneth in 1963 after which the island was again bought privately.

Inch Kenneth seen from Gribun, with Ulva behind.

A decorated coffin cover on Inch Kenneth.

Erisgeir

Erisgeir is a tiny islet, legally part of Inch Kenneth, no more than two acres in extent, which is home to puffins and which has afforded grazing for up to six sheep. It is isolated in the expanse of water bounded by Ulva, the Burgh and the north-west coast of the Ross of Mull. Its only claim on the reader's attention is founded on its central role in a favourite legend.

In medieval times Mull was amongst the widespread possessions of the Macdonalds, Lords of the Isles. During this period the daughter of one of these Macdonalds married the chief of the Maclean clan, then based on the mainland; and when the couple produced their first child Macdonald offered to mark the happy event by giving a parcel of land to his grandchild. The wily Macleans asked if the gift could consist of 'Erisgeir and its isles', and the request, which seemed innocuous, was granted. It soon transpired that the land to be conveyed included not only the surrounding small islands but also Mull itself: and that was how the Macleans achieved their dominant position on Mull.

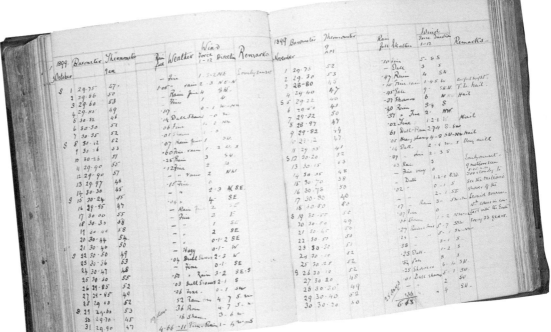

The meteorological records for Inch Kenneth painstakingly kept over many years.

The house on Inch Kenneth.

Staffa

Staffa is remarkable. Its distinctive formation of tall hexagonally-jointed basalt columns imparts an exciting, dramatic quality to the island: and it is this structure that has invited the sea to exploit weaknesses in the rock, forming over the centuries an assortment of caves.

*Inside Fingal's Cave by
William Daniell, 1817.*

Of these caves, Fingal's Cave is known best. The name is, indeed, known around the world. Formed wholly within the columns, with the surging ocean for its floor, and running back over 200 feet into the body of the island, it is unforgettable.

Fingal's Cave has been extolled by Mendelssohn in his Hebrides Overture, made the subject of an oil painting by Turner, and praised in prose and verse by Sir Walter Scott, Wordsworth, Keats, Tennyson, Jules Verne and others.

Clamshell Cave, beside the jetty, with its astonishing wall of lofty curving columns also claims attention; and other caves, which can be only appreciated at low tide in calm weather, have unique features of their own.

Staffa, which is almost a mile long from north to south and about quarter of a mile across, lies six miles north of Iona and eight miles

from the pier at Ulva Ferry. Thanks to its volcanic origin the island supports lush grass over all its plateau-like surface, with neither heather nor bracken present, thereby offering excellent grazing. In the eighteenth century herdsmen and their families lived on Staffa throughout the year to tend the sheep, cattle and other animals kept there. Traces of the difficult life the residents must have been forced to lead can still be seen.

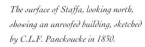

*The surface of Staffa, looking north,
showing an unroofed building, sketched
by C.L.F. Panckoucke in 1850.*

The companion publication *The Island of Staffa* provides more information about the island's geology, history, inhabitants, owners, notable visitors, and its colonies of seabirds. Since 1986 the island has been a property of the National Trust for Scotland.

The tilted colonnade around the southern tip of Staffa, with Fingal's Cave on the right.

Ulva from Ben More, with Gometra just visible to the left.

Eorsa

Eorsa is a rounded featureless island measuring almost a mile by half a mile, in the middle of Loch na Keal. It has the ruins of a cottage on it, and the remains of a long dry stone wall which used to run right across the island. Sheep graze satisfactorily there despite the vigorous bracken. At one time goats were introduced on to Eorsa in an attempt to free the island of adders.

Little Colonsay

The island of Colonsay is 20 miles south of the Ross of Mull: notwithstanding the name, Little Colonsay lying just south of Ulva is apparently unconnected. The latter is much the same size and shape as Eorsa but somewhat more exposed and more evidently formed of volcanic flows. It too has a ruined cottage, and evidence of agricultural work: and like Eorsa it has no sheltered anchorage or landing place. In 1978 the owner built a substantial house on the island.

Ulva and Gometra

Ulva lies only 150 yards off Mull, but it is nonetheless a distinct entity. It is four and a half miles long from east to west and about two miles wide, rising to over 1,000 feet in the centre. The sheltered eastern end of the island is able to sustain a variety of crops and provide good grazing. The name Ulva is derived from the Norse word for a wolf.

Gometra, measuring about one and a half miles each way, is separated from the western edge of Ulva by a narrow cleft, and joined to it by a single-span bridge which carries the unmetalled road from Ulva Ferry and Ulva House to Gometra House and the anchorage. Though not a high as Ulva, Gometra is rugged.

Sir Walter Scott came to Ulva in 1810 and 1814, being put up in an earlier Ulva House on each occasion by the laird, Ranald Macdonald, who was a fellow advocate; and from Ulva he was twice taken to Staffa and Iona. Macdonald was a young, generous and flamboyant host, treating Scott to fusillades of musketry and the constant attention of a personal piper.

Sir Walter Scott.

The silhouette of Ulva seen from many directions exhibits the steps characteristic of land built of successive layers of lava, similar to the trap landscape of the Burgh. On Ulva there are raised beaches and several caves which were long ago formed by the action of the sea but which now are up to 150 feet above high tide. well

A famous son of Ulva was Lachlan Macquarie. (There are many ways of spelling this surname. The version used here is that followed by Lachlan when signing his name.) He was born on Ulva in 1761. He served in the British Army from 1777 until 1809 when, as Major-General Macquarie, he was appointed governor of New South Wales. During the following eleven years he transformed the territory from being a degenerate destination for convicts, riddled with crime and extortion, to a well-administered, prosperous colony. Widely known as 'The Father of Australia', he died on Mull in 1824. He lies in the mausoleum at Gruline, which is safeguarded by the NTS on behalf of the National Trust of Australia.

Visitors are welcome on Ulva. As well as enjoying the grand views, walkers on the island will see the desolate remains of many deserted villages, mostly near the water's edge, showing poignantly how hard the de-population affecting Mull as a whole struck Ulva. The causes were the same, but their effects were exacerbated here by the high proportion of its total income that Ulva derived from the sale of kelp in the early 1800s. In 1840 more than 600 people had their homes on Ulva: in 1847 the number had fallen to 500; and by 1851 it had dropped abruptly to 150. A hundred years later it was down to single figures. Now, happily we can report that, the population is once again growing.

Harp Rock, looking west from high ground on Lunga.

Puffin.

Treshnish Isles

The Treshnish Isles archipelago consists of a six-mile string of sea-eroded lava islets running south-west from a little way off Port Haunn on Mull. Leaving aside the many minor skerries and rocks, there are four points of interest. Starting from the Mull end:

Cairn na Burgh More and Cairn na Burgh Beg were clearly once a single structure but are now divided from each other by a shear-sided breach through which the sea flows. There are the well-preserved remains of military buildings on both. Certainly both were occupied by English troops at the times of the Jacobite rebellions of 1715 and 1745 to deter and, if possible, report upon efforts by the French and the Highlanders to establish contact with one another. There is evidence that the Cairn na Burghs had been identified as natural strongpoints and fortified on various occasions long before - from Norwegian occupation in the fifteenth century.

Razorbill.

Fulmar.

Eider duck on its nest, with Harp Rock on the skyline.

Shags.

Kittiwake feeding chick.

Fladda, as its name might suggest, is little more than a featureless raft of lava. It does have the merit of plentiful and reasonably safe grazing.

Lunga is the biggest of the Treshnish Isles.

Cairn na Burgh More with two of the military structures.

There are ruined black houses on the island, last used as summer shelter for herdsmen in 1857, round-the-year residence having ended in 1824. Sheep are now left to graze there alone, as on other islands. On the western side of Lunga there is a tall, chamfered stack known as Harp Rock. Large concentrations of seabirds including fulmar, shag, kittiwake, guillemot, razorbill and puffin breed there.

Bac Mor, commonly called the Dutchman's Cap, offers a striking profile consisting of a wide flat terrace with a pronounced dome in the middle. Queen Victoria, when sailing past on her way to Staffa in 1847, was sufficiently intrigued by the shape of the island to make a sketch of it in her journal.

Guillemot and chick.

INDEX

Map drawn by Johannes Blaeu,
about 1647.

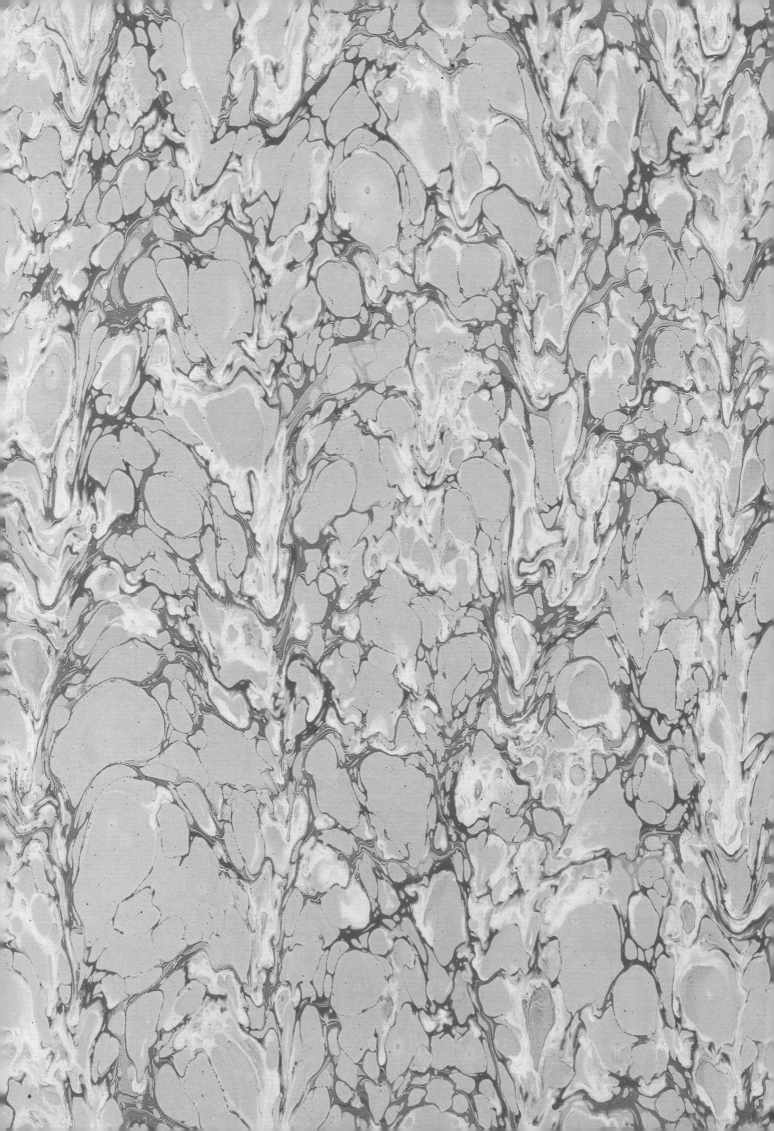